RENDER FLOOR PLANS WITH PHOTOSHOP

Robert H. Frank

ISBN: 9781731008671
For information about permission to reproduce selections
from this book, email robert@rfassoc.com

Book Design by Lauren Frank
Editing by Joan Frank

TABLE OF CONTENTS

INTRODUCTION

Not everyone has the ability to read plans and clearly understand the design intent of an architectural project. The purpose of this book is to give those with the task of creating presentation and marketing documents the skills to render floor plans that are visually understandable and have more impact.

Rendered plans can be accomplished using traditional media such as watercolor, marker, or color pencil. As this book will show using Adobe Photoshop as the rendering medium will allow you to imply 3-dimensional qualities to a 2-dimensional line drawing. The biggest advantage to using Photoshop is having the ability to adjust and change materials quickly. As many of us know in the design field know, changes are inevitable and part of the design process.

There is more than one way to render with Photoshop. The techniques shown here are how I use the application; you may find that other steps are more suited to your workflow. My hope is that you will be able to use this book as a guide to rendering your own plans.

This book is meant as a resource for both students and professionals in the fields of interior design, architecture, and graphic design. Some of you will have more experience than others. I have written this book so that the first paragraph describes the steps and the second more detailed information; primarily more detail on using the tools.

Lastly, I have tried to simplify the process as much as possible, using only 13 of the 66 tools available to render a floor plan. Any version of Photoshop CS and up will have the same tools and panels used in this book, though the appearance of some of the icons may look different. The Adobe website is the best place to start for detailed instructions on all of Photoshop tools.

https://helpx.adobe.com/support/photoshop.html

PHOTOSHOP INTERFACE

This section gives you a basic description of the workspace and vocabulary used in this book. As you follow each step of this book you will become more familiar with Photoshop tools and interface as they pertain to rendering floor plans.

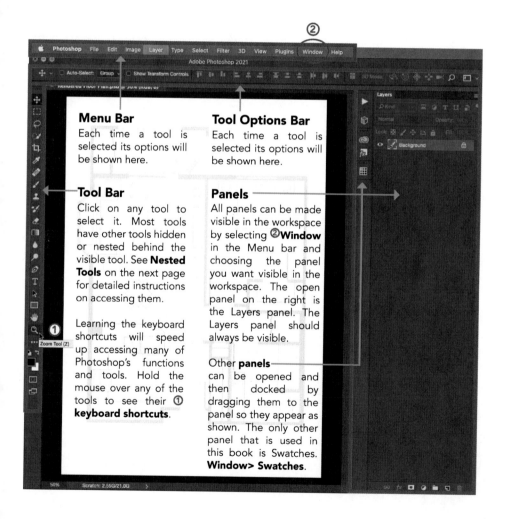

Menu Bar
Each time a tool is selected its options will be shown here.

Tool Options Bar
Each time a tool is selected its options will be shown here.

Tool Bar
Click on any tool to select it. Most tools have other tools hidden or nested behind the visible tool. See **Nested Tools** on the next page for detailed instructions on accessing them.

Learning the keyboard shortcuts will speed up accessing many of Photoshop's functions and tools. Hold the mouse over any of the tools to see their ① **keyboard shortcuts**.

Panels
All panels can be made visible in the workspace by selecting ②**Window** in the Menu bar and choosing the panel you want visible in the workspace. The open panel on the right is the Layers panel. The Layers panel should always be visible.

Other **panels** can be opened and then docked by dragging them to the panel so they appear as shown. The only other panel that is used in this book is Swatches. **Window> Swatches**.

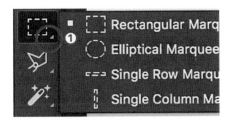

Nested Tools

To access nested tools click on the ①**small arrow** located at the bottom right corner of the tool. The above image shows the Selection tools nested within the Rectangular Marquee Tool.

Nested tools relate to each other. For example the Rectangular Marrque tool will have three other marquee tools nested within it.

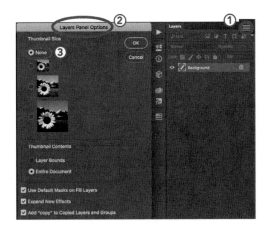

Layers Panel

Clicking on the ①**hamburger icon** at the top right corner of the Layers panel will give you access to the ②**Layers Panel Options**. There you can change the layer icons to ③**None** (this is the setting used in this book) or a thumbnail. I use None as it takes up less space in the Layers Panel.

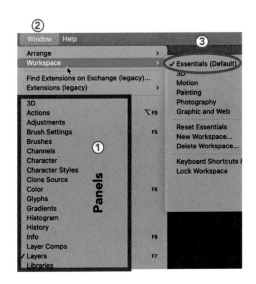

Workspace

All of the ①**Panels** can be accessed by going to ②**Window> Workspace**.

The default workspace is ③ **Essentials**. Click on the others if you would like to see other workspace options.

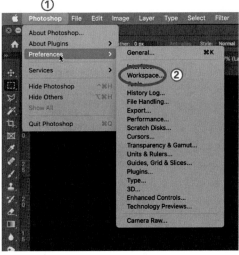

Preferences

Changes can be made to the look of your workspace by selecting ①**Photoshop> Preferences>**②**Workspace...**(Mac) or **Edit> Preferences> Workspace...** (Windows) from the menu bar.

FILE TYPES

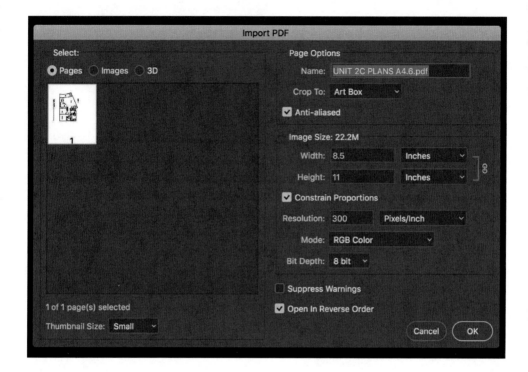

Vector Files

Vector files are created in CAD programs such as AutoCad and Vectorworks as well as Adobe Illustrator. The only vector files Photoshop can open are EPS, PDF, and AI (Adobe Illustrator). Therefore you must save the CAD file as an EPS or PDF file; PDF is the most common. See your application instructions on how to save a PDF file.

When opening a vector file in Photoshop the above dialog box will appear.

Set the image size to what the final print size will be. To print up to 11x17 300 Pixels/Inch is ideal. For larger sizes 144 Pixels/Inch will often suffice without any noticeable loss of image quality.

Bitmap Files

Bitmap or raster files are image files that in the simplest terms will get pixelated (jagged edges) if they get enlarged too much. See the lower right image.

If you are going to work with a plan that has been scanned or photographed it will be a bitmap image file such as JPEG or TIFF. Since these file types do not enlarge without losing quality it is best to scan the plan at the desired print size. For example at 11x17, 300 dpi.

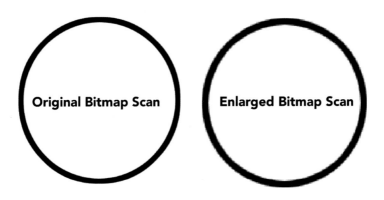

1

WOOD FLOORS

If you would like to use the floor plan and patterns in this book, download the resource files at **rfassoc.com/book.html**. Choose **File> Open** from the menu bar to open a floor plan.

If you are working with a vector file, it will open with a transparent background. To flatten the image so it appears as shown, select ①**Layer>** ②**Flatten Image** from the menu bar.

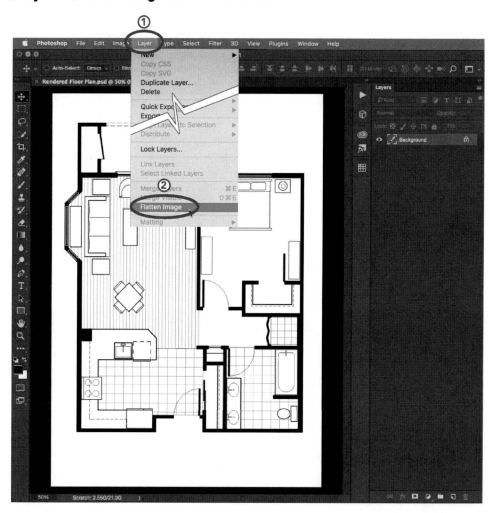

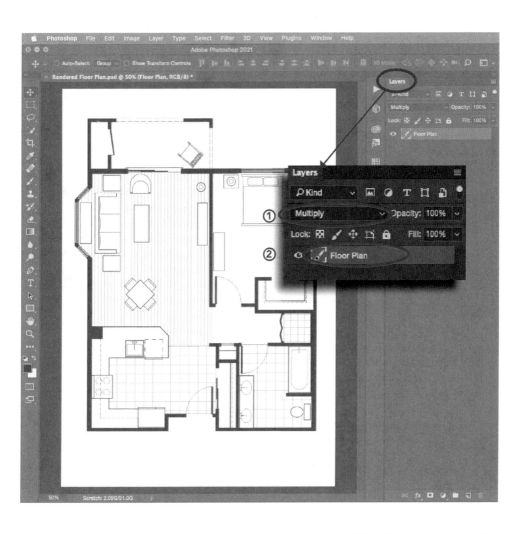

Change the layer blending mode to ①**Multiply**. Rename the Background layer to ②**Floor Plan**.

Click on the blending mode name in the Layers panel to activate the pull down menu, drag down to select ①**Multiply**. This will allow any layer below the floor plan layer to be visible. Double clicking on the ②**layer name** will allow you to type in a new name.

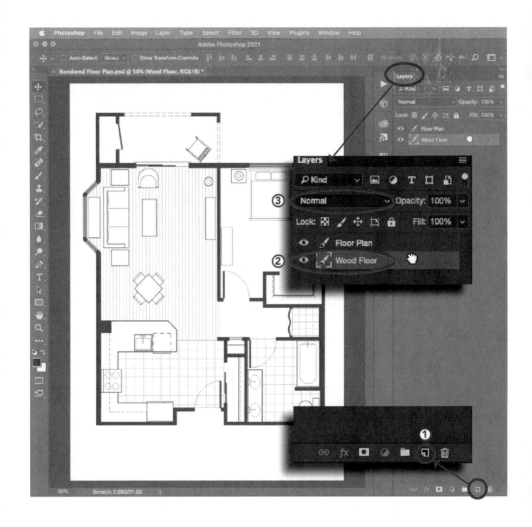

Create a new layer. To create a new layer click on the ①**new layer icon**. Label it ②**Wood Floor**. Move the layer below the Floor Plan layer. Keep the blending mode set to ③**Normal**.

To move the layer click on the layer name and drag it down so it is below the Wood Floor layer.

Choose the ①**Rectangular Marquee tool** 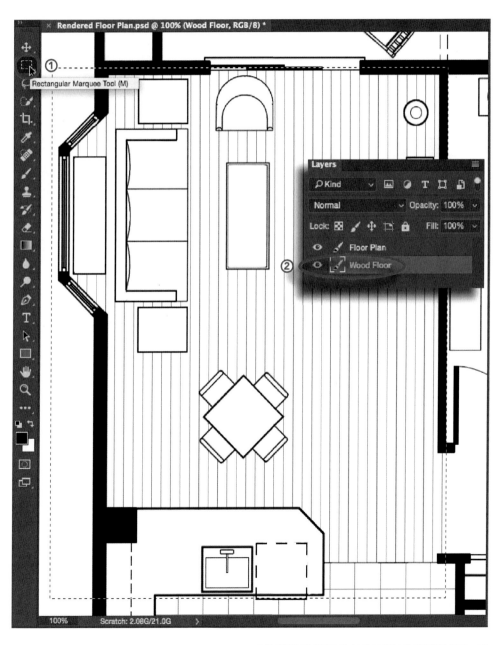 and create a rectangular selection that goes outside the boundaries of the wood floor. Make sure the ②**Wood Floor layer** is selected in the Layers panel.

If the Rectangular Marquee tool is not visible then click on the small arrow in the lower right corner of the tool as illustrated on page 7.

Select a color to be used for the wood floor.

Double click on the ①**Set Foreground Color** swatch. Move the sliders and/or pick a color within the ②**color field**. You can type in the values as shown below to match the color in the ③**new** box. Then click ④**OK**.

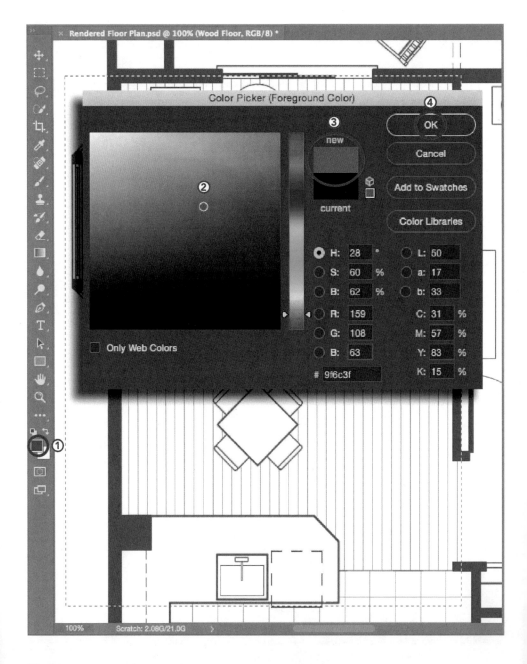

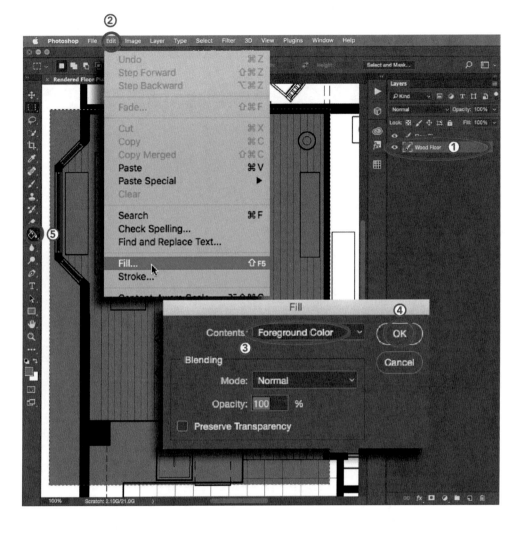

Making sure the ①**Wood Floor layer** is still selected, fill the rectangular selection with the foreground color.

Select ②**Edit> Fill...** Use the contents pull down menu to select ③**Foreground Color**. Use the settings shown above. Then click ④**OK**.

The ⑤**Paint Bucket tool** can also be used to fill the selection. There is often more than one way to get the same results in Photoshop.

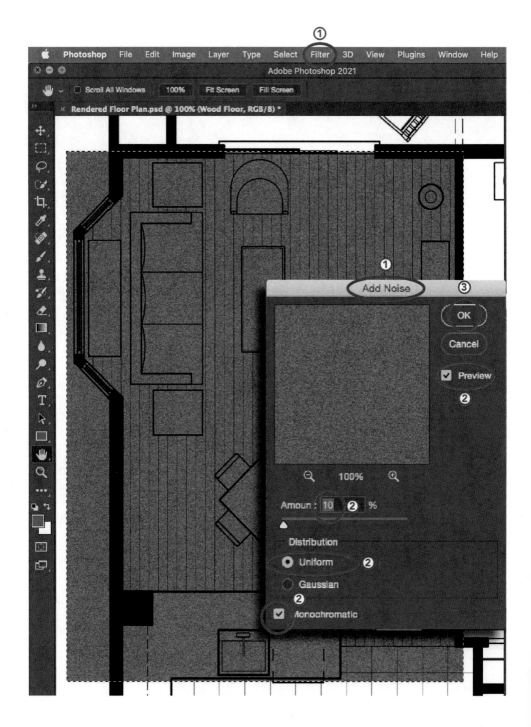

Select ①**Filter> Noise> Add Noise...** Use the ②**settings** above as a starting point. The amount of noise should not be too strong. The more noise the larger the wood grain will appear when proceeding with the next step. Then click ③**OK**.

Select ①**Filter> Blur> Motion Blur...** Use the settings shown below to create the wood grain. The ②**angle** needs to be set parallel to the floorboards. ③**Distance** determines the length of the blur. Then click ④**OK**.

When using Motion Blur the top and side edges will have an anomaly that we don't want in the rendering, that is why the selection is made larger than the room.

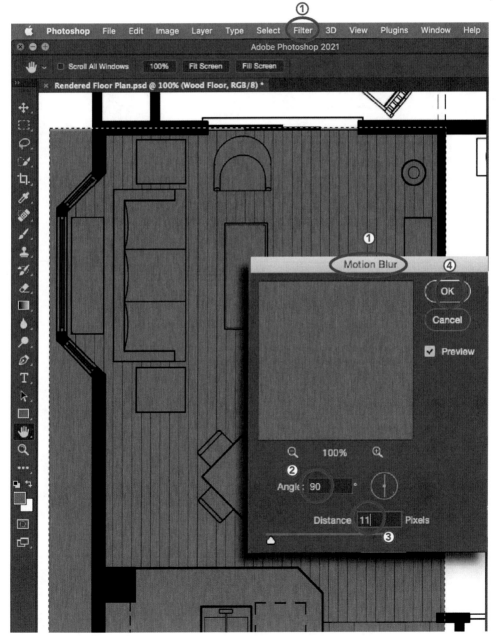

Use the ①**Polygonal Lasso tool** and follow the floor outline as shown below. Next choose ②**Select> Inverse**. Press the delete key to erase the floor area outside of the selection.

To use the ①**Polygonal Lasso tool** click once and hold down the shift key to constrain the lasso in a vertical, horizontal, and 45 degree angle. Click around the edges. When you get to the starting point the cursor will change shape ,click one last time.

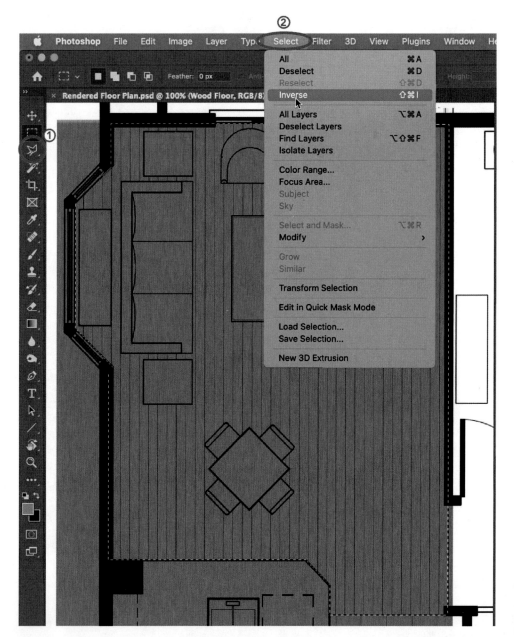

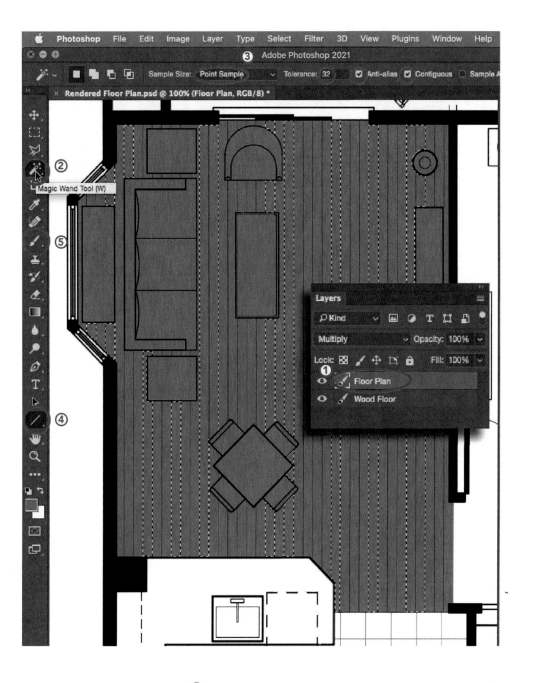

Select the ①**Floor Plan layer** in the layers panel. Using the ② **Magic Wand tool** click on a few randomly spaced floor boards. Use the settings shown in the ③**Tool Options bar**.

The ②**Magic Wand tool** will only select closed shapes. If there are breaks in the lines you'll need to use the ④**Line** , ⑤ **Brush** , or ⑤**Pencil** tool to close the break(s) before using the Magic Wand tool.

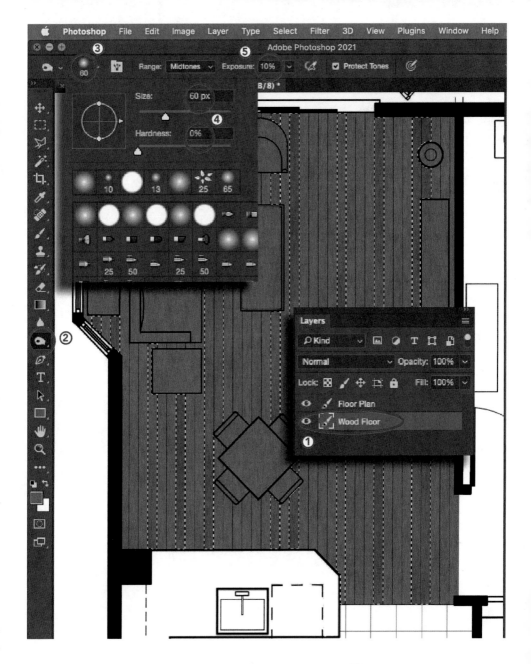

To make some of the floorboards darker. Select the ①**Wood Floor layer** in the layers panel. Then select the ②**Burn tool** . In the tool options bar click on the ③**Brush Preset Picker;** select a ④**large soft brush;** set the ⑤**exposure** to a low number. Click and drag the ②**Burn tool** parallel to the floorboard within the selected areas.

Using the bracket keys on the keyboard will also change the brush sizes. The left key will make the brush smaller and the right larger.

To make the lighter floorboards use the brush settings used for making the darker floorboards except use the ①**Dodge tool** , which is nested within the Burn tool, to make some of the floorboards lighter.

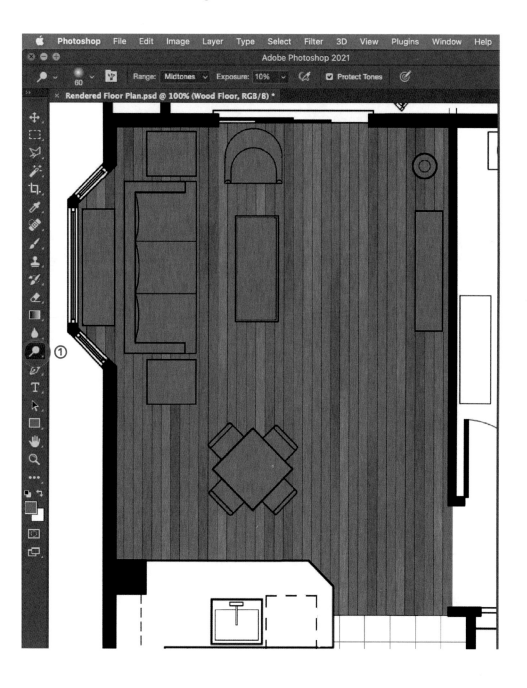

FABRIC PATTERNS

Open a seamless pattern or use this one from **rfassoc.com/book**. Many can be found by doing a Google image search for seamless fabric pattern. Then go to ①**Select> All** then ②**Edit> Copy**.

An image that can be placed side-by-side without creating a boundary or seam between the copies of the image is a seamless texture. There are many seamless patterns that can be downloaded from the Web.

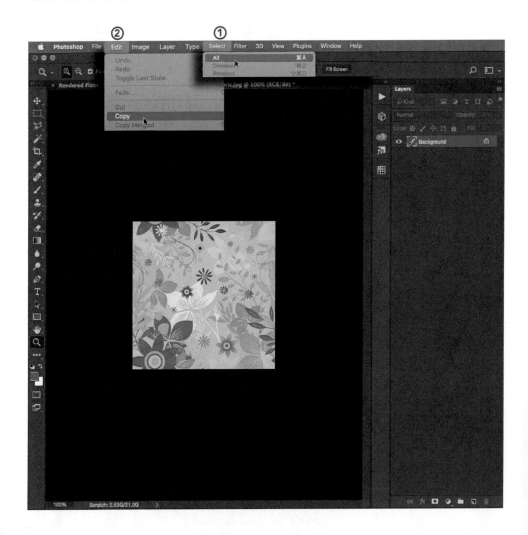

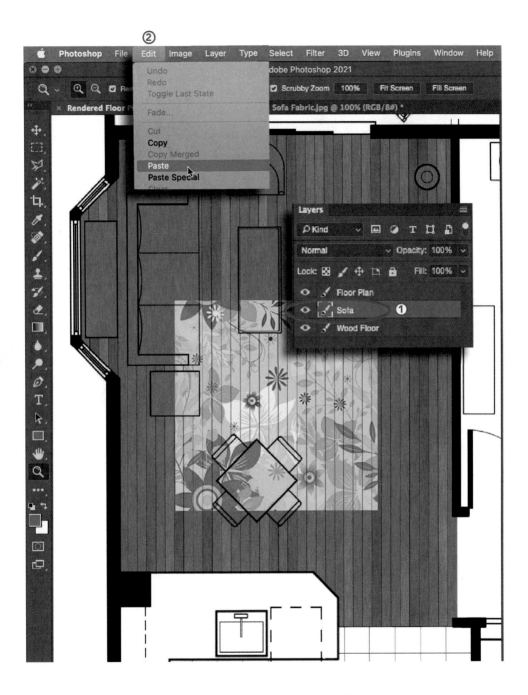

Go back to the rendered floor plan file. Create a new layer and label it ①**Sofa**. Place it above the Wood Floor layer. Choose ②
Edit> Paste to paste the pattern.

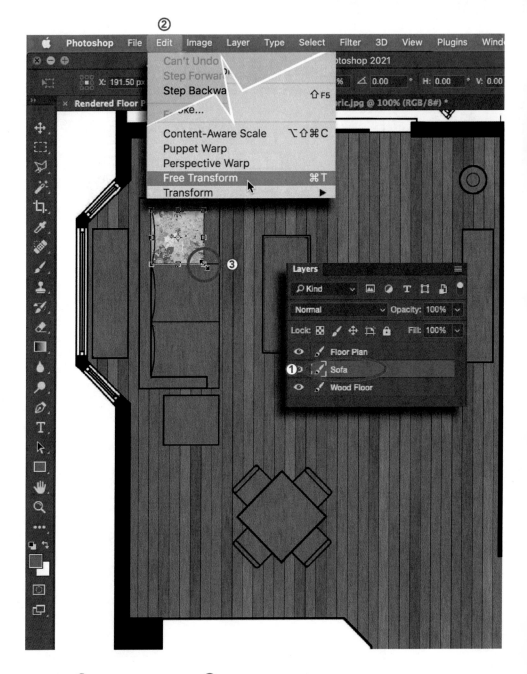

With the ①**Sofa** layer selected, ②**Choose Edit> Free Transform**. Grab one of the ③**corner handles**, click and drag to scale the pattern to the desired proportions.

If you need to enlarge the pattern it will most likely become blurry. Choose one that is the correct size or larger. Holding down the shift key constrains the proportions while scaling the image. See - https://helpx.adobe.com/photoshop/using/transforming-objects.html

Hide the ①**Floor Plan** and ①**Wood Floor layers** by clicking on the eye icon next to the layer's name. Then use the ②**Rectangular Marque tool** and carefully select the pattern so the selection is exactly on the edge of the fabric pattern.

In order to make an accurate selection you may need to magnify the pattern. Use the ③**Zoom tool** to do this. Using Select> All will not work when we go to the next step defining the pattern.

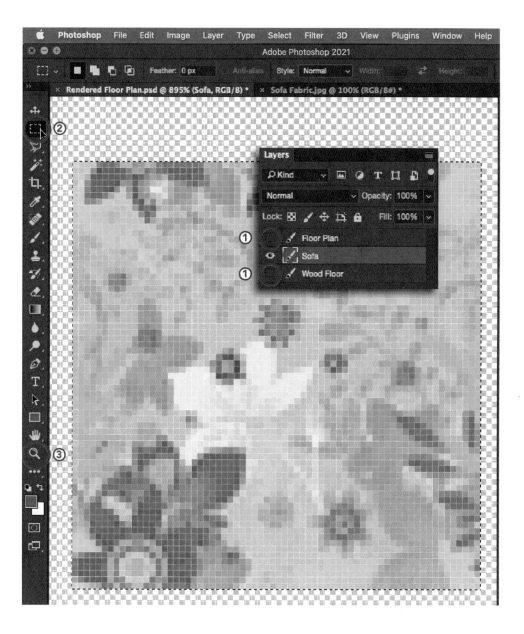

Choose ①**Edit> Define Pattern**. ②**Name the pattern Sofa Fabric**. ③**Click OK**.

Using the ①**Rectangular Marquee tool** ▢ make a selection around the sofa. Make sure the ②**Sofa layer is selected in the Layers panel**. Choose ③**Edit> Fill...** Under the ④**Contents pull down menu select Pattern**. Click on ⑤**Custom Pattern.** ⑥**Choose the pattern you just created** and click ⑦**OK**.

All of the patterns that come with Photoshop and the ones you create will always be available here for future projects.

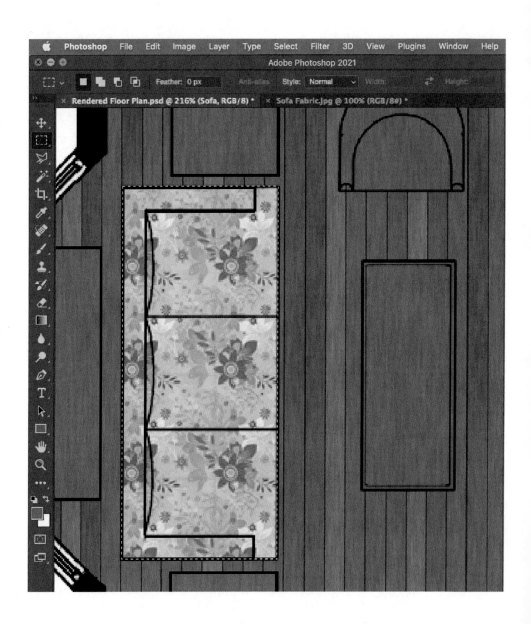

This is the seamless pattern placed on the sofa.

SHADING & HIGHLIGHTS

With the ①**Floor Plan layer selected** use the ②**Magic Wand tool** 🪄 to select the seat cushions. Hold down the Shift key when clicking on each of the 3 cushions. Select the ③**Sofa layer** and use the ④**Burn tool** 🖐 to add shading to the cushions. Use a low ⑤**exposure setting** and ⑥**soft brush** to gradually build up the values

For this rendering the light will be coming from the upper left. Therefore the shading will be on the ⑦**bottom and right side of each cushion**.

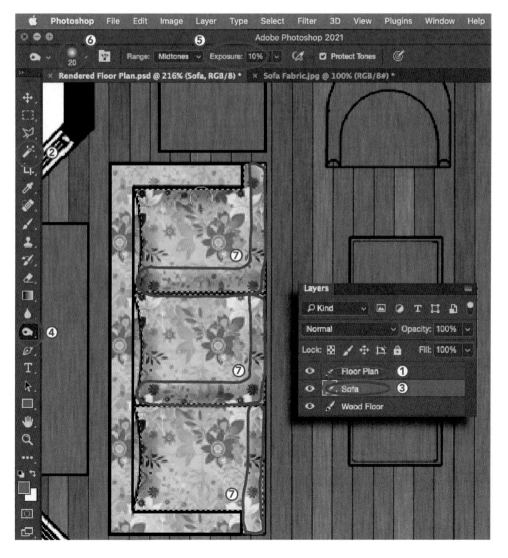

Keeping the cushions selected as shown in the previous step, use the ①**Dodge tool** 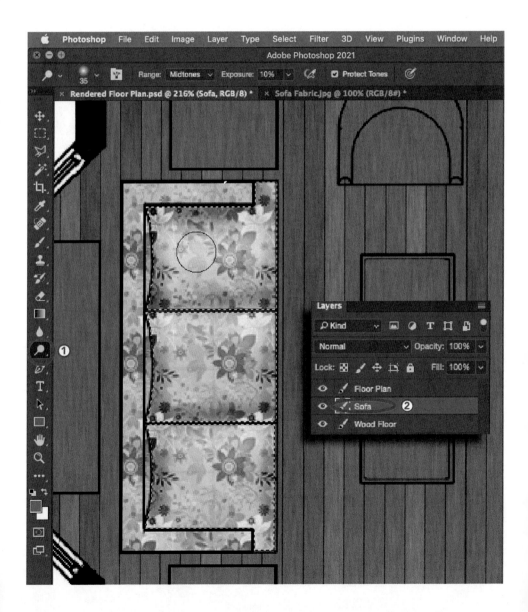 to lighten the upper portion of the cushions.

As with the Burn tool use a low exposure setting and soft brush to gradually lighten the values. Make sure the ②**Sofa** layer is selected.

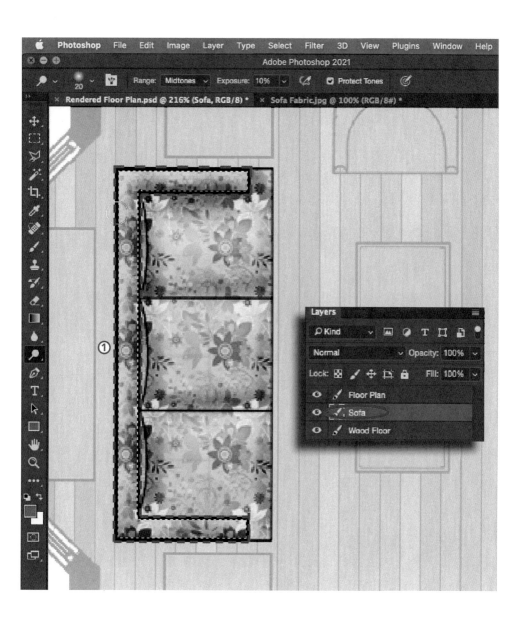

Using the same steps for adding shading and highlights to the cushions, do the same for the ①**sofa back and armrests**. This will complete the rendering of the sofa.

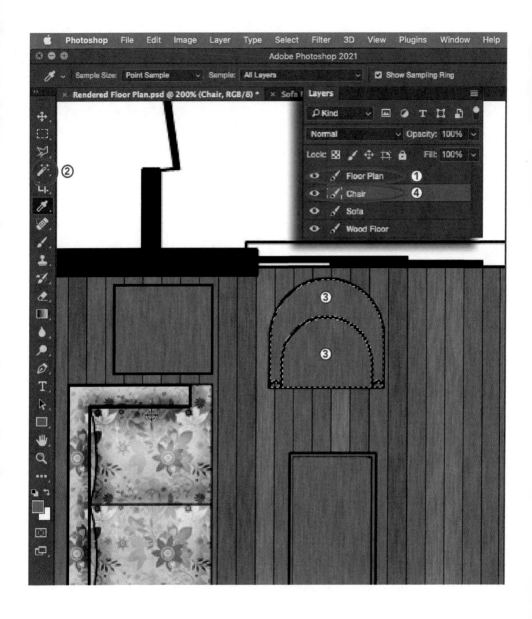

Click on the ①**Floor plan layer** and then with the ②**Magic Wand tool** ✨ click on the ③**two spaces within the chair** while holding down the shift key. Make a new layer and label it ④**Chair**.

Another way to make a new layer is by choosing Layer> New> Layer... from the menu bar.

Click on the ①**Chair layer**. Create a ②**foreground color** (see page 16 showing how to pick colors). Choose ③**Edit> Fill**. In the Contents pull-down menu choose ④**Foreground Color.** Click ⑤ **OK**.

A selection can also be filled by using the ⑥**Paint Bucket tool**. After the selection is made click inside the selection with the Paint Bucket tool.

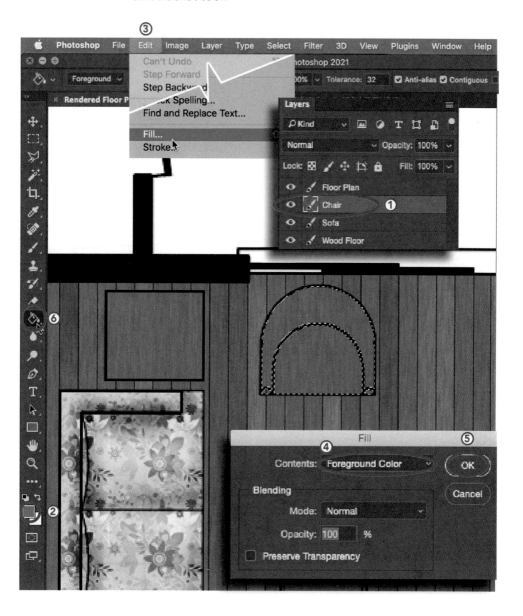

Use the ①**Burn** 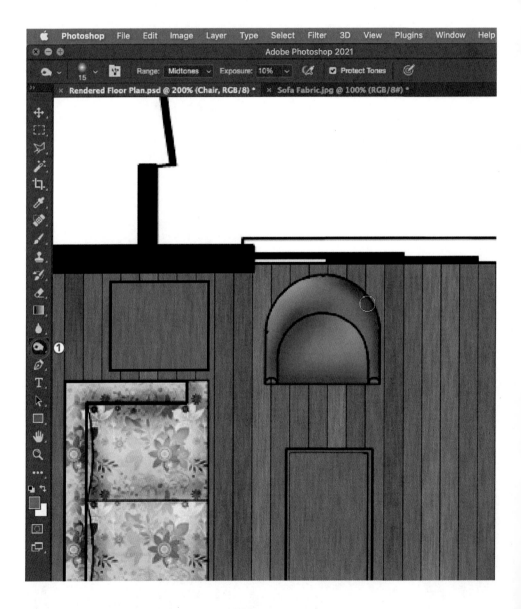 and ①**Dodge** **tools** (these tools are nested together) on the Chair layer to render it. The rendering steps are the same as shown for the sofa.

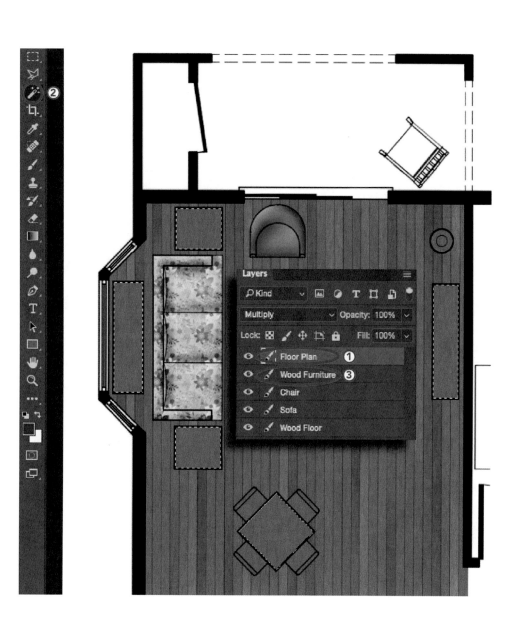

Select the ①**Floor Plan layer.** Using the ②**Magic Wand tool** click on the shapes that will become the wood furniture. Hold down the shift key as you click on each piece. Make a new layer and label it ③**Wood Furniture**.

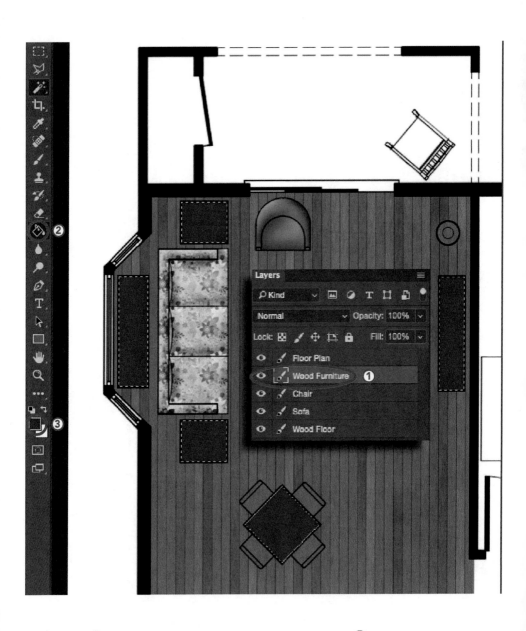

Select the ①**Wood Furniture layer**. Using either the ②**Paint Bucket tool** or Edit> Fill.. from the menu bar, fill the selection with the ③**foreground color**.

Page 16 shows how to choose a foreground color.

Use the ①**Burn** and **Dodge** **tools** to lightly add light and dark variations to the wood furniture. Make sure the ②**Exposure** setting in the tool options bar is set to a low number such as 10%.

When using the Burn and Dodge tools on a light color, the exposure settings need to be higher. Use low exposure settings for dark colors and higher for light.

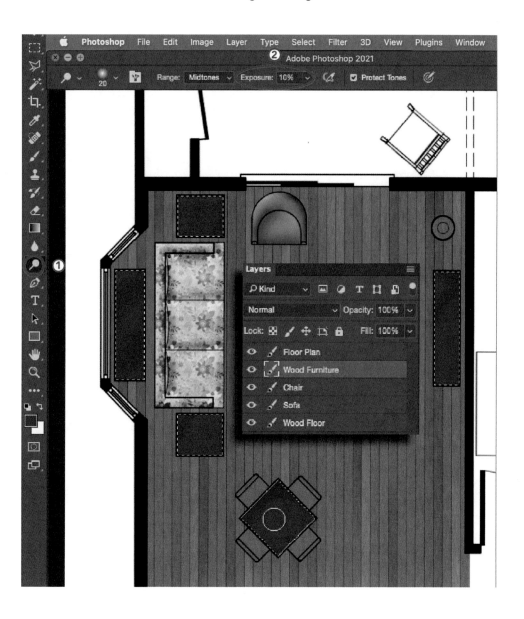

Select the ①**Floor Plan layer**. Use the ②**Magic Wand tool** and click inside of the ③**dining chairs**. ④**Create a new layer** and **label it Dining Chairs**.

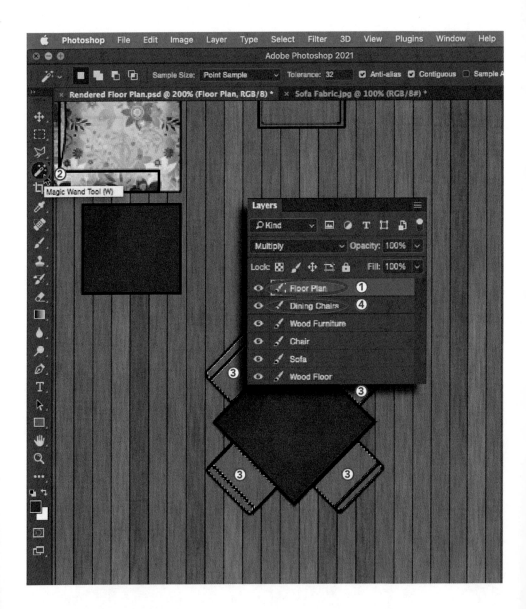

①**Select a foreground color** and then using the ②**Paint Bucket tool**  or Edit> Fill... from the menu bar, fill the selected chairs with the foreground color. Make sure the ③**Dining Chairs** layer is selected in the layers panel.

Select the ①**Floor Plan layer**. Use the ②**Magic Wand tool** and click inside each seat on the dining chairs while holding down on the shift key. Select the ③**Dining Chairs layer**. Use the ④**Burn tool** to render shadows on the chair seats.

GRADATIONS

Select the ①**Floor Plan layer**. Use the ②**Magic Wand tool** ✨ and click inside of the ③**lamp shade**. ④**Make a new layer and label it Lamp**. Double click on the ⑤**Background Color Swatch** and pick a light color. Then click ⑥**OK**.

Double click on the ①**Set Foreground Color Swatch** and pick a darker color than the background color. Then click ②**OK**.

The foreground and background colors can be interchanged by clicking on the ③**double arrow arc icon** above the large swatches.

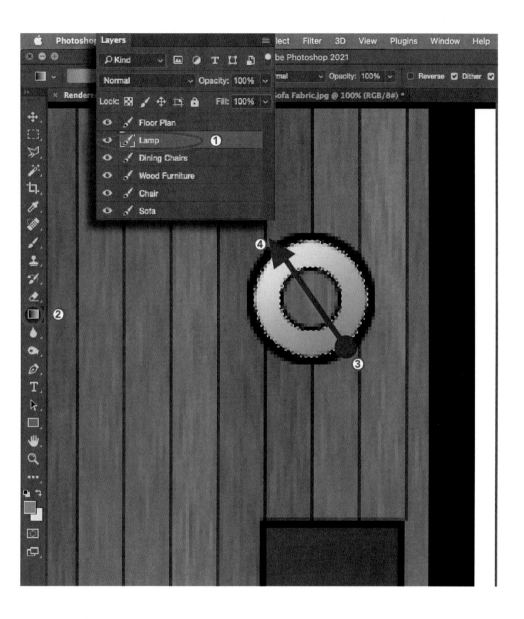

Click on the ①**Lamp layer**. Use the ②**Gradient tool** 🔲 to create the curved effect of the lamp shade.

To use the ②**Gradient tool** 🔲 click on the ③**starting point** and drag the rubber band to the ④**end point**. The starting point will be the foreground color, where it ends is the background color.

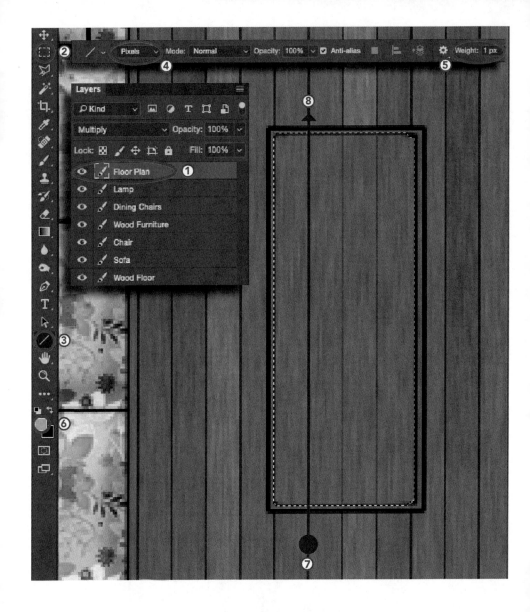

GLASS TABLETOP

First we need to add the missing floor lines not drawn in the plan. Select the ①**Floor Plan layer**. Use the ②**Rectangular Marquee tool** and make a rectangle where the glass will be rendered. Click on the ③**Line tool** . Make sure the pick tool mode is set to ④**Pixels** and ⑤**Weight 1**. Select a light grey ⑥**foreground color**.

Add the missing lines using the ③**Line tool** . Click at the ⑦ **starting point,** hold down the shift key to constrain its vertical direction, drag to the ⑧**end point** and release. Since the area is selected you can start and end the line outside of the selection.

Make a new layer, label it ①**Glass Table Top**. Choose a color for the glass in the ②**Foreground Color Swatch**. With the Glass Table Top layer selected fill the area with the foreground color.

Use the ③**Paint Bucket tool** or Edit> Fill..., Foreground Color from the menu bar to fill the selected area.

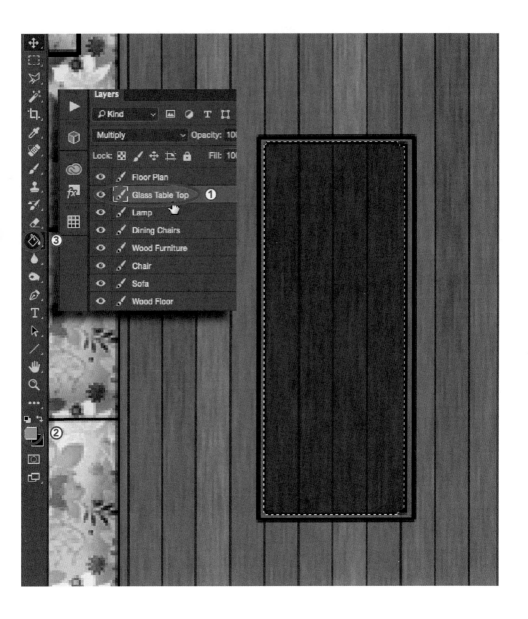

Keep the glass portion selected. Make a new layer and label it ①
Glare. Click on the ②**Brush tool** . In the Brush tool options
bar select a large ③**soft brush**, ④**Mode-Normal**, and ⑤**Opacity
20%**. The ⑥**foreground color** should be white. Click on a few
spots to render ⑦**reflected light**.

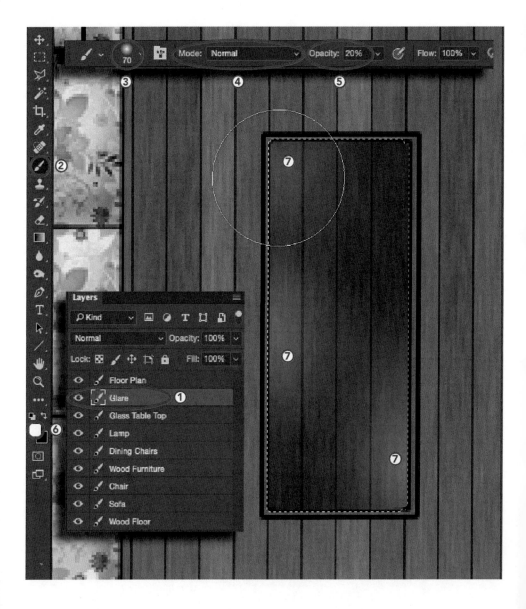

Make a new layer, label it ①**Table Frame**. Click on the ②
Rectangular Marquee tool 🔲 and make a selection around
the entire table. Hold down the command and option keys (Mac)
or ctrl and alt keys (Windows) while clicking on the ③**Glass Table
Top** layers thumbnail or small paintbrush icon. This will subtract
the glass so just the frame is selected. Then fill the ①**Table
Frame layer** with a light grey ④**foreground color** using the ⑤
Paint Bucket tool 🪣.

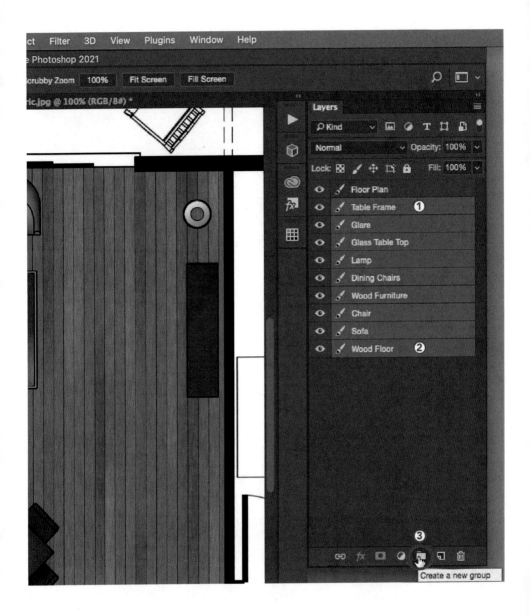

LAYER FOLDERS

First select all of the layers below the Floor Plan layer by clicking on the ①**Table Frame** layer.   Then hold down the Shift key and click on the last layer – ②**Wood Floor** to select multiple contiguous layers.   Click on the ③**Create a new group icon** at the bottom of the layers panel.

To select multiple noncontiguous layers, Ctrl-click (Windows) or Command-click (Mac OS) on the individual layer names.

All of the layers previously selected will now be in a new folder. Name the folder ①**Living/Dining**.

When you have a project with a lot of layers it's helpful to keep them organized in folders. Clicking on the folder eye icon will hide all of the layers within it. Clicking on the arrow next to the folder will open and close it.

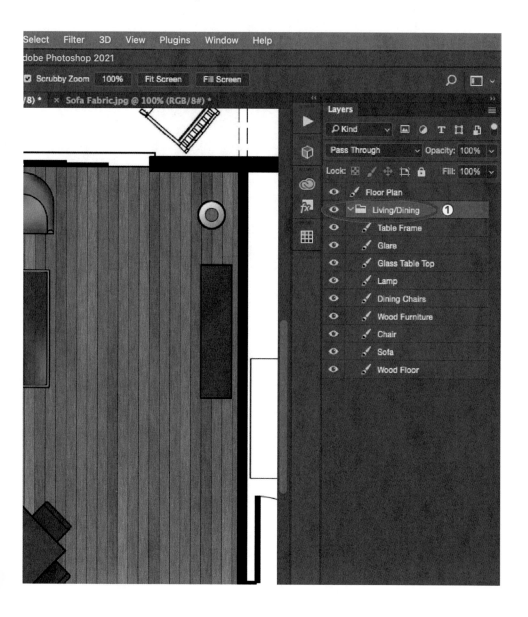

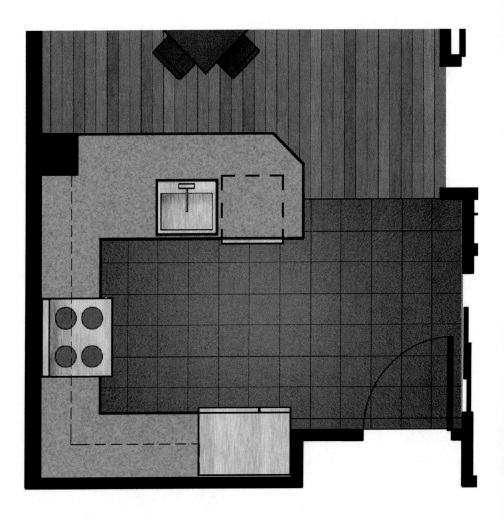

2

STONE COUNTERTOP

Make a new layer and label it ①**Countertop**. Use the ②**Magic Wand tool** 🪄 or ③**Polygonal Lasso tool** 🪢 to make a selection around the countertop. Fill the selection with ④**white foreground color**.

Instructions on how to use the ③Polygonal Lasso 🪢 tool are on page 20.

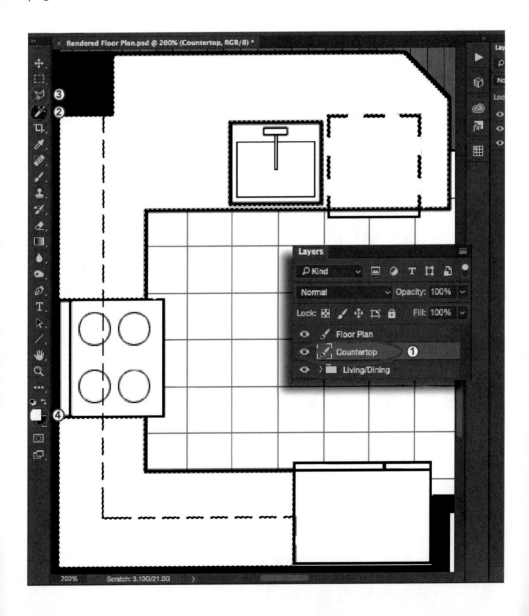

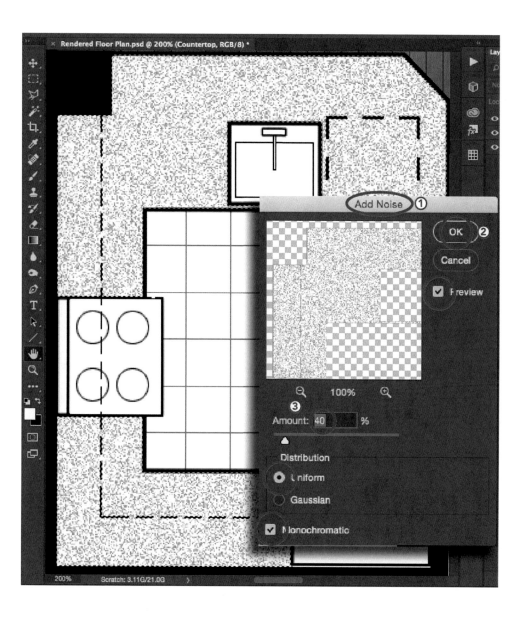

Choose **Filter> Noise> Add Noise...** from the menu bar. Use the settings shown above in the ①**Add Noise** dialog box and click ②**OK**.

This will give the base for the countertop texture. Higher ③ **Amount** settings will increase the grain.

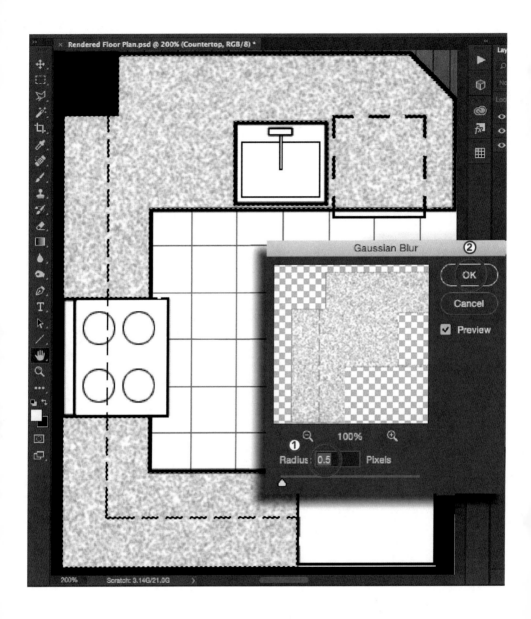

Choose **Filter> Blur> Gaussian Blur..** from the menu bar. Set the
①**Radius to 0.5** and then click ②**OK**.

Use a low ①**Radius** setting. The higher the number the more
blurry the grain will become. Experiment with different settings
to get different looks.

Color the counter by choosing **Image> Adjustments> Hue/ Saturation...** from the menu bar. Place a check mark next to ① **Colorize**. Move the ②**Lightness** slider to the left to add a darker value. Then use the ③**Saturation** and ④**Hue** sliders to apply and adjust color. When you are satisfied with the results click ⑤**OK**.

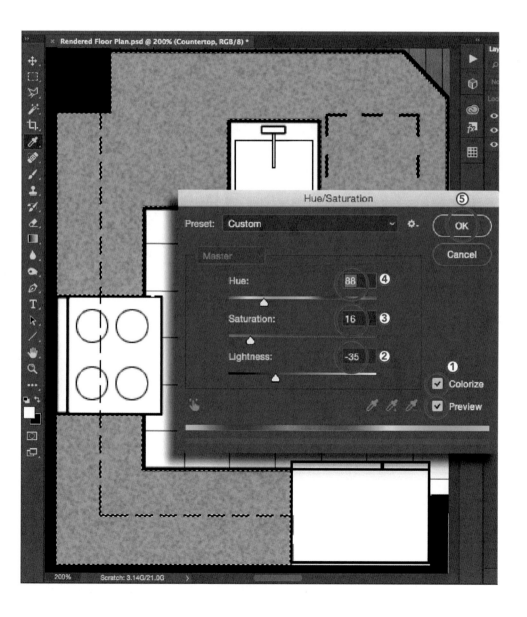

TILE FLOOR

Make a new layer and label it ①**Tile Floor**. Using the ② **Rectangular Marquee tool** 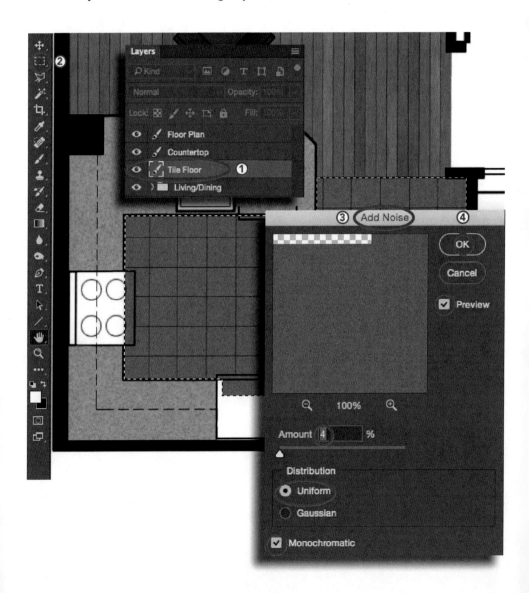, make a selection around the kitchen floor. Choose **Filter> Noise> Add Noise...** from the menu bar. Use the settings shown in the ③**Add Noise** dialog box. Click ④**OK**.

To add to the selection hold down the Shift key (Mac & Windows), subtract from the selection hold down the Option key (Mac) or Control key (Windows) while using any of the ②**selection tools**.

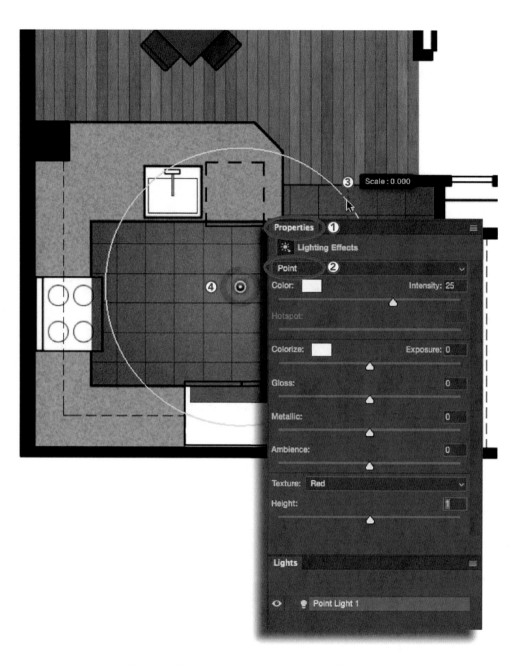

Choose **Filter> Render> Lighting Effects...** from the menu bar. The ①**Properties** panel will appear allowing you to choose the type of light and appearance settings. Choose ②**Point**. The size of the light can also be adjusted by placing the arrow on the outside ③**green edge until it turns yellow**. Click and drag to change the light size. The light intensity can also be changed by clicking and dragging the ④**center black ring**.

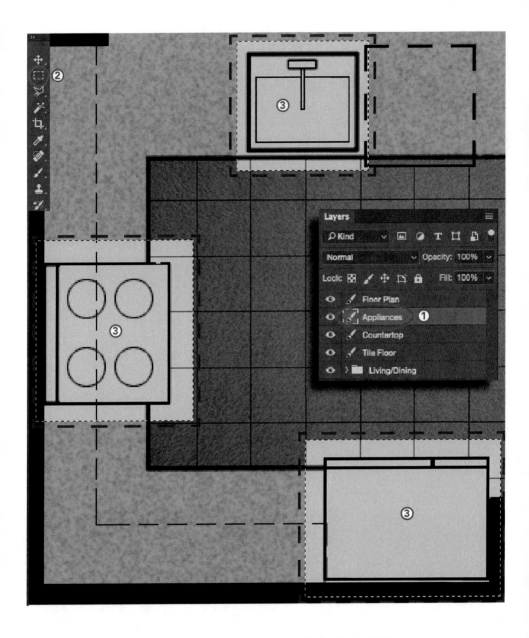

STAINLESS STEEL

Make a new layer and label it ①**Appliances**. Using the ②
Rectangular Marquee tool , make an oversized selections
around the ③**sink, range, and refrigerator**.

Hold down the shift key as you make a selection around each
appliance so they are all selected together.

Choose **Filter> Noise> Add Noise...** from the menu bar. Use the setting shown in the ①**Add Noise** dialog box. Click ②**OK**.

The size of the image will determine what ideal noise amount should be used. Large image sizes will require more noise and smaller image sizes, less.

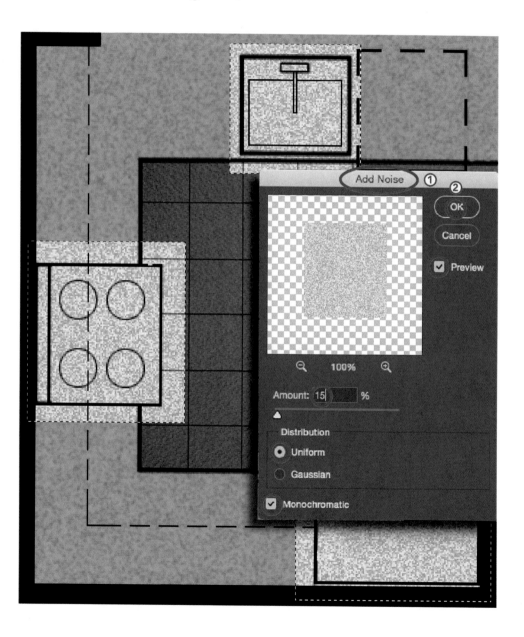

Choose **Filter> Blur> Motion Blur...** from the menu bar. Use the
setting shown in the ①**Motion Blur** dialog box. Click ②**OK**.

Rotating the ③**angle** will change the direction of the motion
blur. Holding down the shift key while rotating the angle icon will
constrain the motion to 15 degree increments.

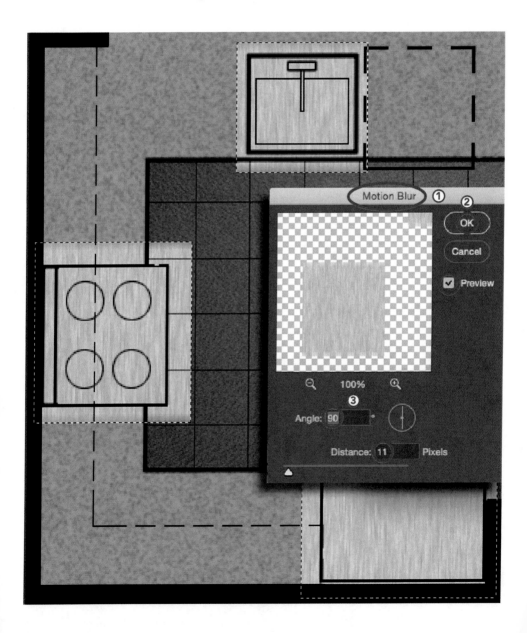

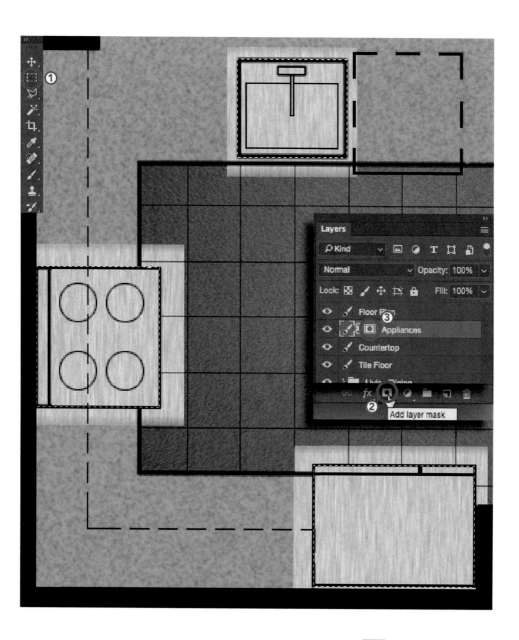

Using the ①**Rectangular Marquee tool** , make a selection within the sink, range, and refrigerator while holding down the shift key. Click on the ②**Add layer mask icon** located at the bottom of the Layers panel.

The ③**layer mask icon** will now appear in the layer name and only the area contained within the selection will be visible as shown on the next page.

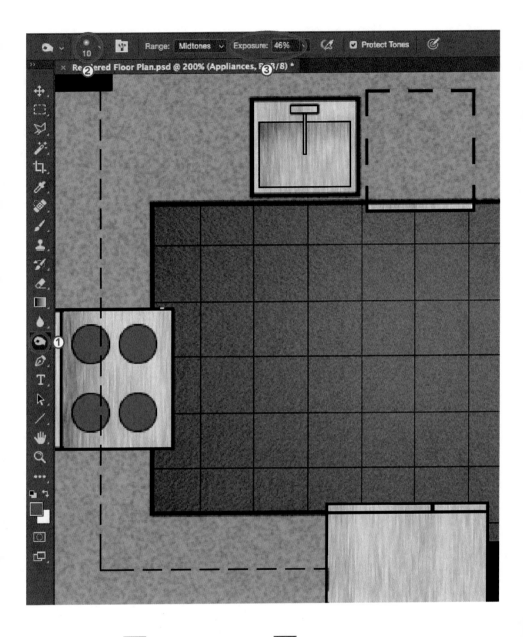

Use the ①**Burn** 🔲 and ①**Dodge tools** 🔲, (these tools are nested together) a ②**soft brush**, and ③**medium exposure setting** to create dark and light value variation on the stainless steel.

When working with dark images use a low ③**exposure** setting (5-10%) to gradually adjust the values.

Lastly, select each of the kitchen layers in the Layers panel. Click on the ①**Create a new group icon** located at the bottom of the layers panel. Label the group ②**Kitchen**.

For step-by-step instructions on creating grouped layers see pages 50-51.

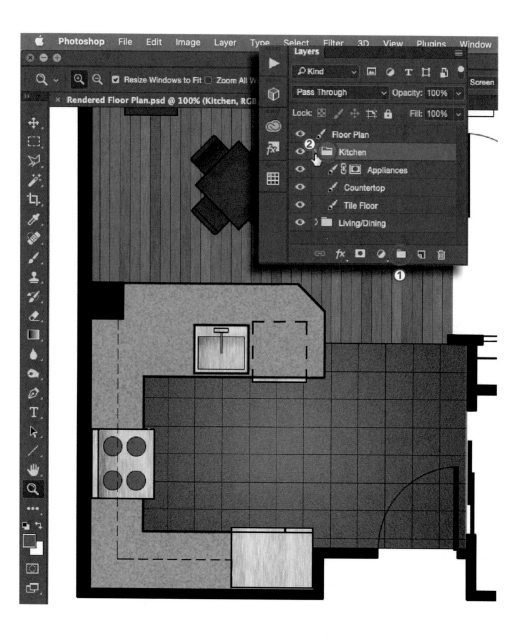

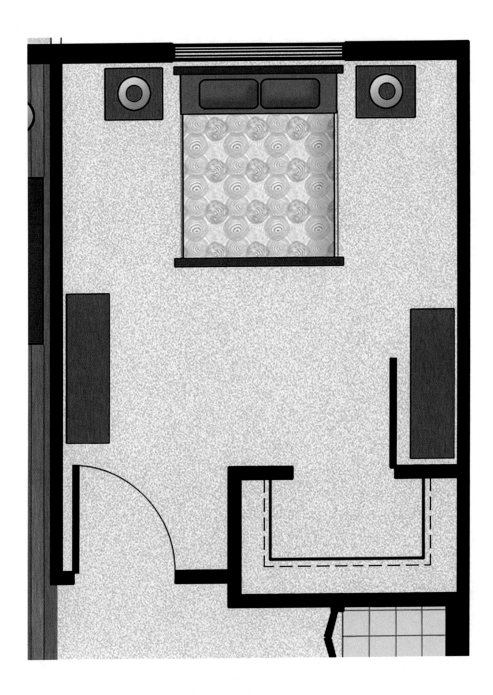

3

CARPET

Make a new layer and label it ①**Carpet**. Using the ②**Rectangular Marquee Tool** ▢, make a selection similar to what is shown with the ③**red dashed lines**. It's okay to have the selection include the walls.

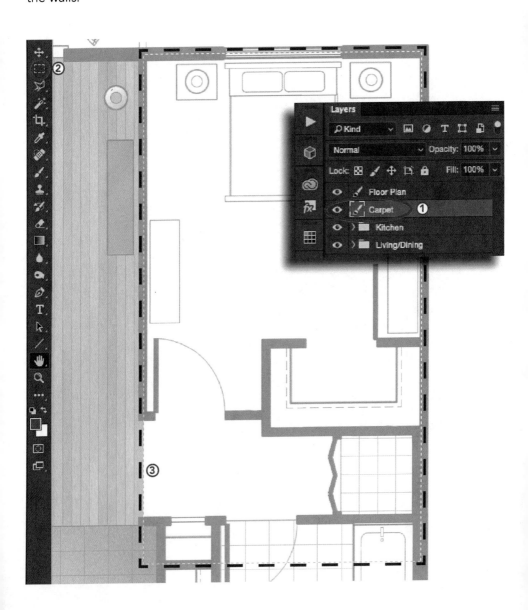

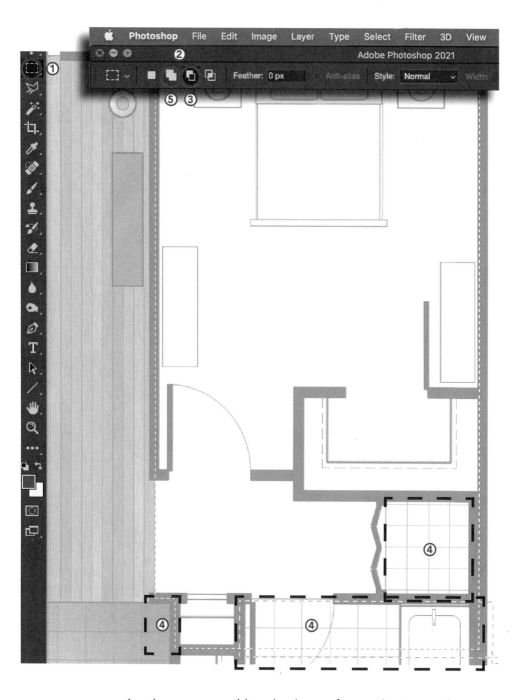

Another way to add and subtract from selections is by using the respective option in the Tool Options Bar. Select the ① **Rectangular Marquee tool** 📷 and then in the ②**Tool Options bar** click on the ③**Subtract from selection** icon. Click and drag the ①**Rectangular Marquee tool** 📷 to remove the selections from the tile floor shown with the ④**red dashed lines**. To add to a selection click on the ⑤**Add to a selection** icon.

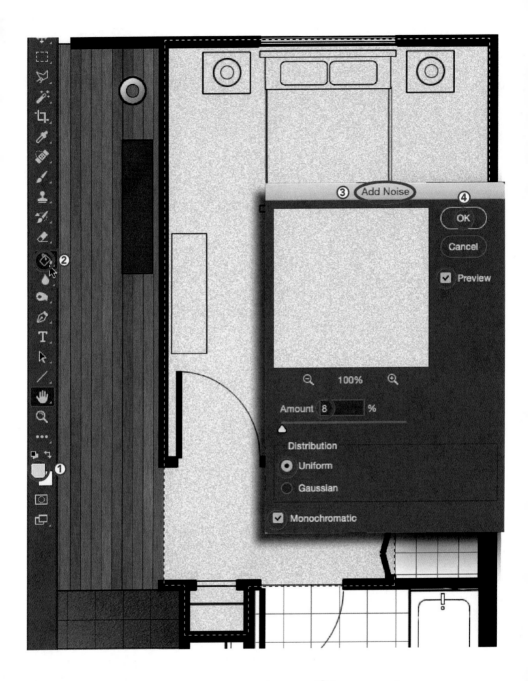

Make sure the selection is still showing. Choose a ①**foreground color**. Select the ②**Paint Bucket tool** 🪣 and fill the selection with the ①**foreground color**. To add a carpet texture choose **Filter> Noise> Add Noise...** from the menu bar. Use the settings shown in the ③**Add Noise** dialog box. To soften the noise choose **Filter> Blur> Blur** from the menu bar. Click ④**OK** when done.

WOOD FURNITURE

Create a new layer and label it ①**Wood Furniture**. Using the ②**Rectangular Marquee tool** , make an oversized selection around the wood furniture. Fill the selections with the desired wood color chosen from the ③**Foreground color swatch;** using the ④**Paint Bucket tool** .

Choose **Filter> Noise> Add Noise...** from the menu bar. Use the settings shown in the ①**Add Noise** dialog box. Click ②**OK** when done.

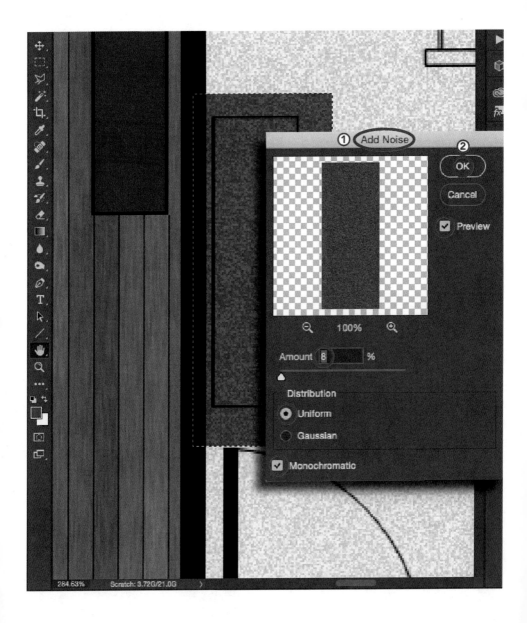

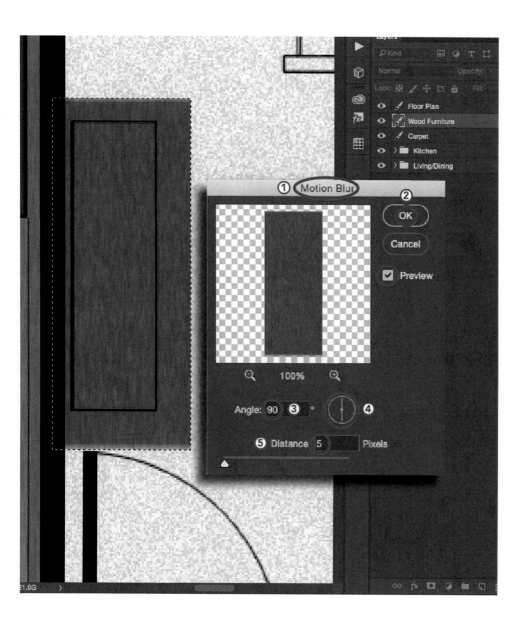

To make the wood grain choose **Filter> Blur> Motion Blur...** from the menu bar. Use the settings shown in the ①**Motion Blur** dialog box.. Click ②**OK** when done.

If you want the grain to be rendered at a different angle enter a specific angle in the ③**Angle** box or click and rotate the ④ **direction tool.** The higher the pixels in the ⑤**Distance** setting increases the length of the grain. This is very similar to how the wood floors were rendered.

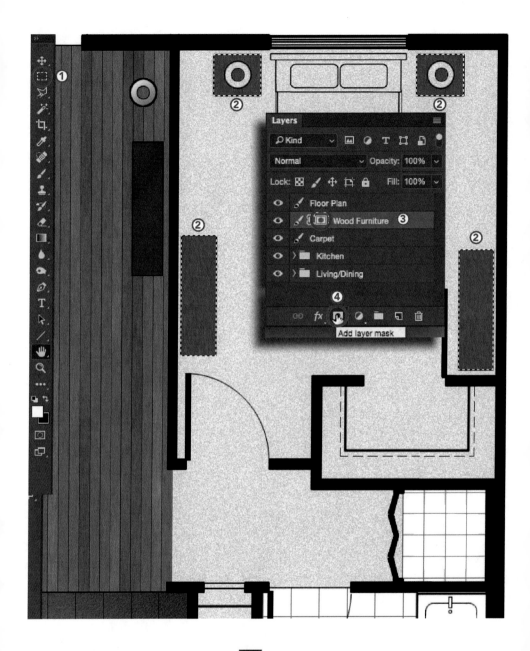

Using the ①**Rectangular Marquee** 🔲 tool make a selection around each ②**wood furniture piece**. With the ③**Wood Furniture layer** selected in the layers panel click on the ④**Add layer mask** at the bottom of the layers panel. This will hide the wood grain that goes beyond the furniture, as the above image shows.

RENDER FABRIC

Create a new layer and label it ①**Sheets, Head & Baseboard**. Using the same steps shown in ②**Chapter 1, pages 24-29, create a pattern** to be used for a bedspread.

The pattern used here can be downloaded from **rfassoc.com/ book**.

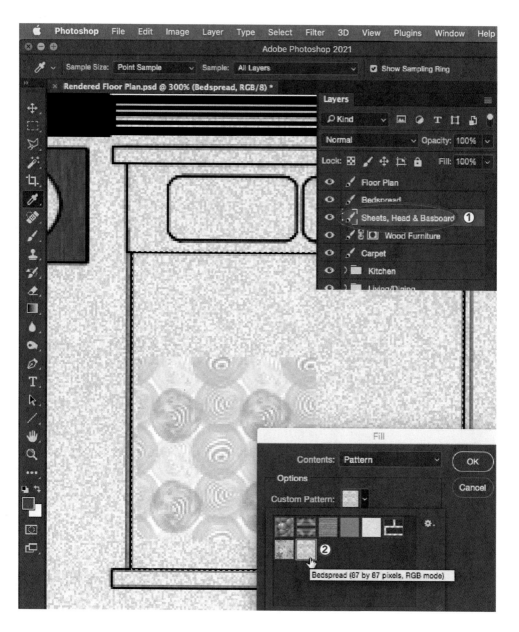

Using the ①**Rectangular Marquee tool** [ ], make a selection around the bed and choose ②**Edit> Fill...** from the menu bar. In the ③**Contents pull-down menu choose Pattern**. Click on the ④**bedspread pattern**. Click on ⑤**OK** to fill the selection with the pattern.

Using the ①**Rectangular Marquee tool** [ ], make a selection around the head and baseboards. Fill using the ⑥**Paint Bucket tool** [ ]. Do the same with the sheets and pillows.

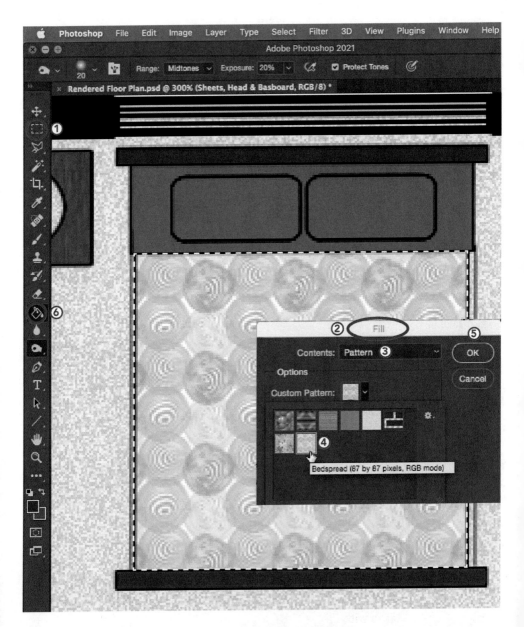

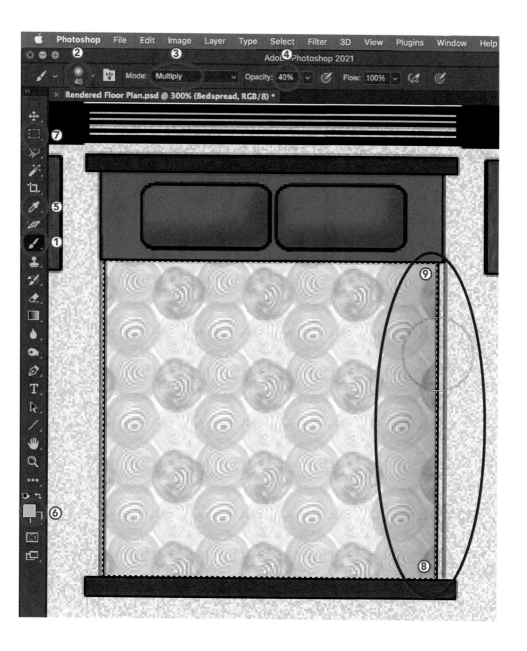

Another method for shading is to use the ①**Brush tool** . In the Tool Options bar select a ②**large soft brush**, change the ③**Mode to Multiply**, and set the ④**Opacity to 40%** or lower. Using the ⑤**Eyedropper tool** select a ⑥**foreground color** from the pattern, use one of the darker colors.

Make a selection around the bed using the ⑦**Rectangular Marquee tool** . Click once on the ⑧**bottom right corner,** hold down the shift key and click again on the ⑨**top right corner** of the bed. This will evenly distribute the shade color. Do the same with the pillows.

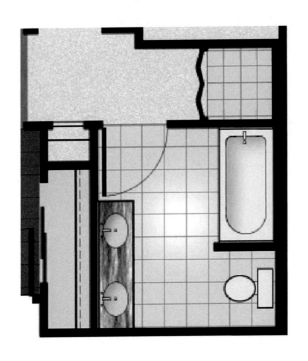

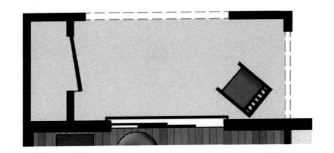

78

4

GRANITE

Create a new layer and label it ①**Bath Vanity**. Using the ②
Rectangular Marquee tool 🔲 click and drag to make a
selection around the entire vanity. Fill the selection with a solid
color using the ③**Paint Bucket tool**. Make the ④**foreground
color black** and the **background white**. Then choose ⑤**Filter>
Render> Clouds**.

This will create a mottled appearance. Each time you use the
Clouds filter a different mottled pattern will appear.

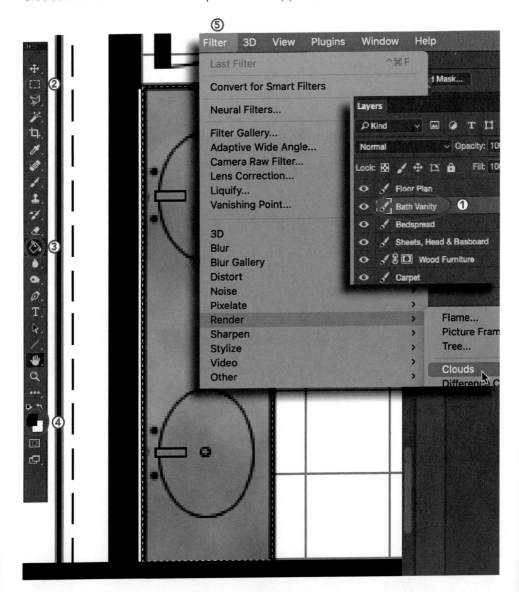

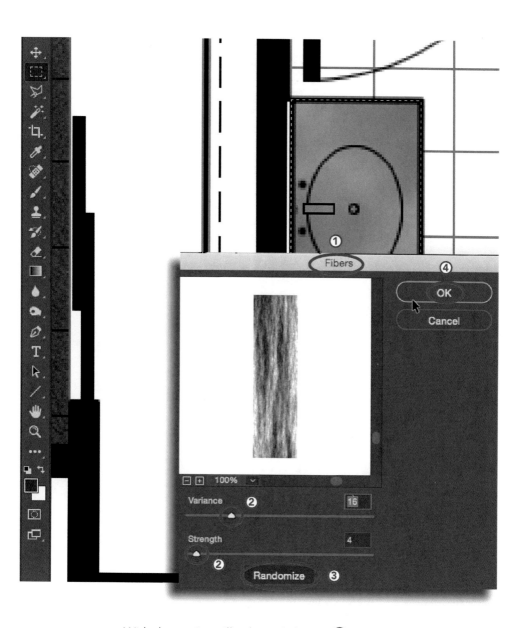

With the vanity still selected choose ①**Filter> Render> Fibers...** Change the appearance of the fibers using the ②**sliders** shown in the dialog box. Click on the ③**Randomize** button to see different fiber combinations. When done click on ④**OK** to see the completed granite texture.

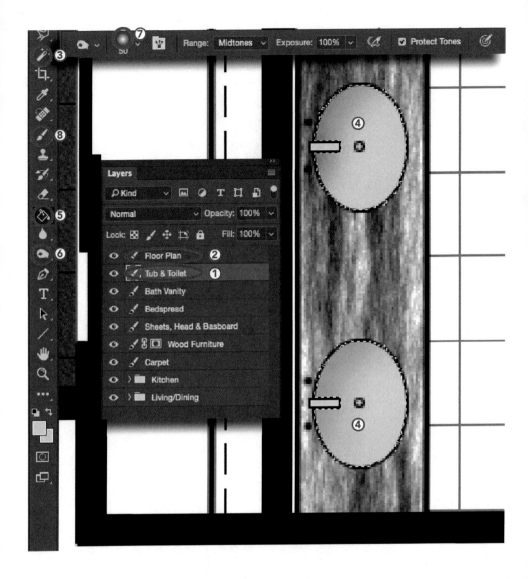

PORCELAIN

Create a new layer and label it ①**Tub &Toilet**. Click on the ②
Floor Plan layer. Using the ③**Magic Wand tool** click inside
the ④**sinks** while holding down the shift key to select each sink at
the same time. Select the ①**Tub & Toilet layer** and fill with a light
grey color using the ⑤**Paint Bucket tool**. Then with the ⑥**Burn
tool** and a ⑦**large soft brush** add shading to the inside of
the sinks.

If you have pure white sinks you will need to paint the shading
with the ⑧**Brush tool** as shown on page 77. The Burn and
Dodge tools will not have any effect on pure white.

Using the exact same steps outlined for rendering the sinks, render the ①**tub** and ②**toilet**.

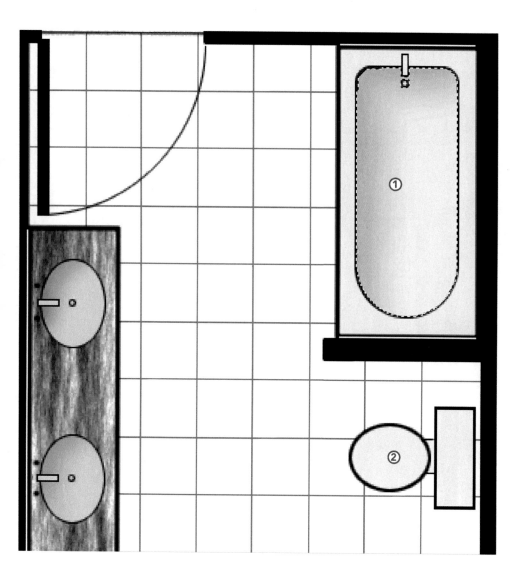

FLOOR TILE

Create a new layer and label it ①**Floor Tile**. Select the ②
Rectangular Marquee tool 🔲 and make a selection around
the entire floor. It's okay to include the walls. Fill the selection with
a color using the ③**Paint Bucket tool** 🪣.

To make the reflection use the ④**Dodge tool** 🔍 and ⑤**large
soft brush.** Click once or twice in the middle of the floor to render
highlights.

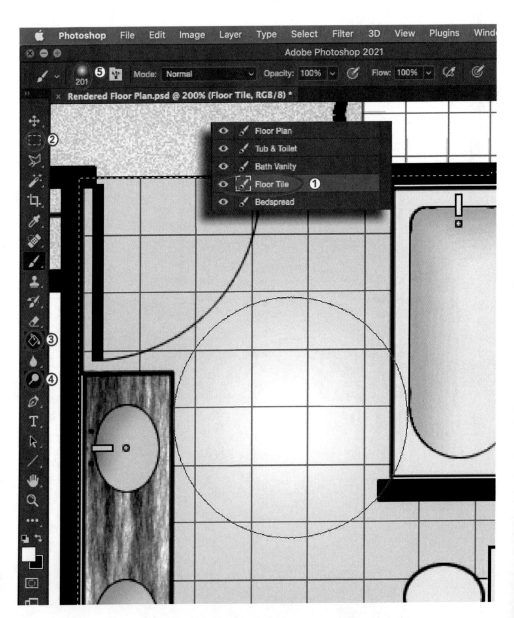

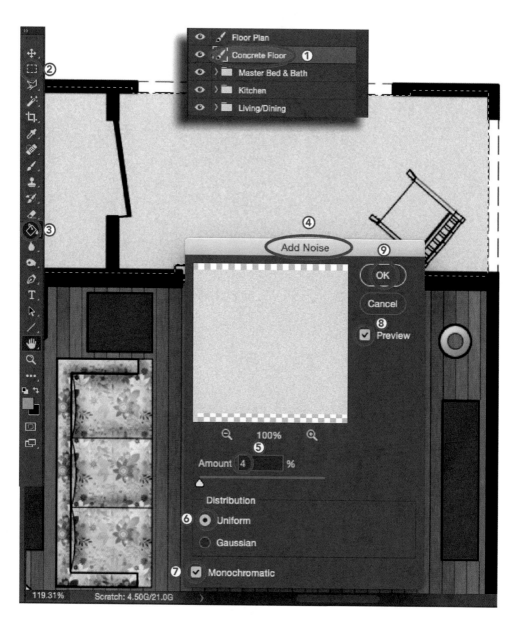

CONCRETE

Create a new layer and label it ①**Concrete Floor.** Using the ②
Rectangular Marquee tool [icon] make a selection around the
patio floor. Fill the selection with a light grey color using the ③
Paint Bucket tool [icon]. Use ④**Filter>Noise>Add Noise...** from
the menu bar. For a rough appearance use a high percentage
in the ⑤**Amount number box**, a lower number will imply a
smoother surface. Choose ⑥**Uniform** and ⑦**Monochromatic**.
Place a check mark next to ⑧**Preview** so you can see the effects
in the Add Noise panel. Click ⑨**OK** when done to see the
concrete patio floor.

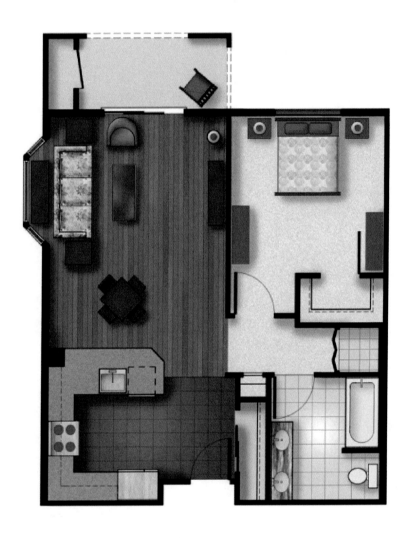

5

SHADOW LAYERS

Create a new layer in the ①**Living/Dining folder** and label it ②
Shadows. Place it above the Wood Floor layer. Set the blending
mode to ③**Multiply** by selecting from the pull-down menu.

Do this for each room, placing the shadow layer above the floor
layer and below the furniture layers.

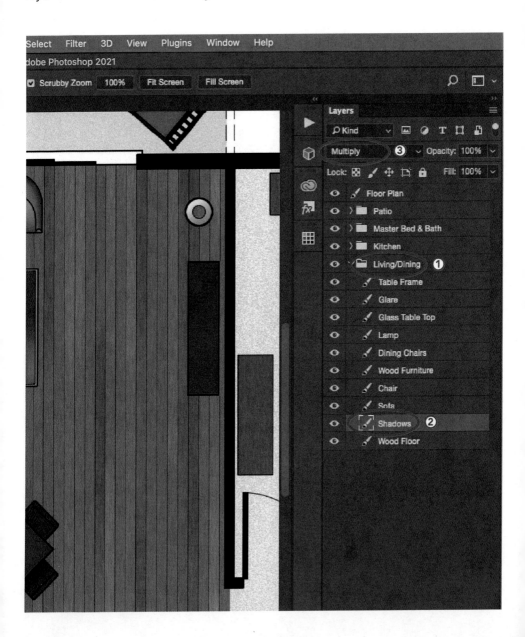

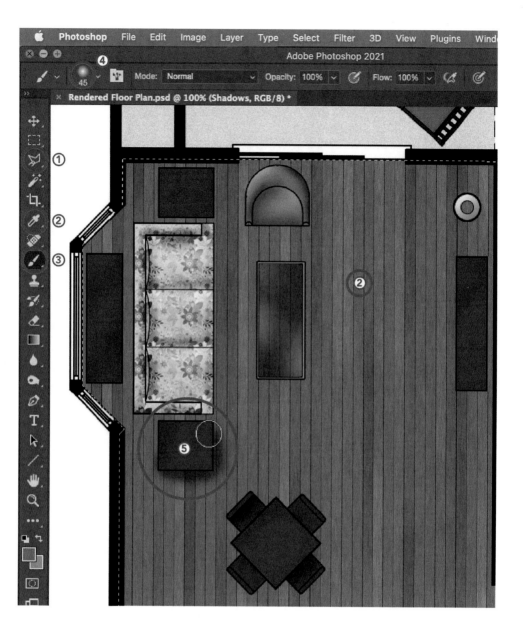

RENDER SHADOWS

Make a selection around the Living/Dining area Using the ①
Polygonal Lasso tool . Using the ②**Eye-Dropper tool**
pick a ②**color from the floor**. Use the ③**Brush tool** with a
④**large soft brush** and paint along the two sides of the objects
that would cast the shadows, as shown for the ⑤**end table**.

Always cast the shadows coming from the same direction. For
this plan the shadows will be cast with the light coming form the
top left.

CLEAN UP SHADOWS

Use the ①**Eraser tool** and a ②**soft brush** to clean up the shadows. Click and drag to erase the corners at a 45 degree angle, indicated by the black double arrows.

SHADOWS ON DARK SURFACES

Use the same steps for rendering shadows on the wood floor shown on pages 89-90 for the other rooms.

Since the counter is slightly higher than the furniture the ①**Brush Tool** size is slightly larger at ②**50 pixels**. To avoid having the shadows too dark on a dark floor, use a slightly lighter color of the floor or other surface receiving the shadow. For the kitchen floor shadow use the ③**lighter floor color**.

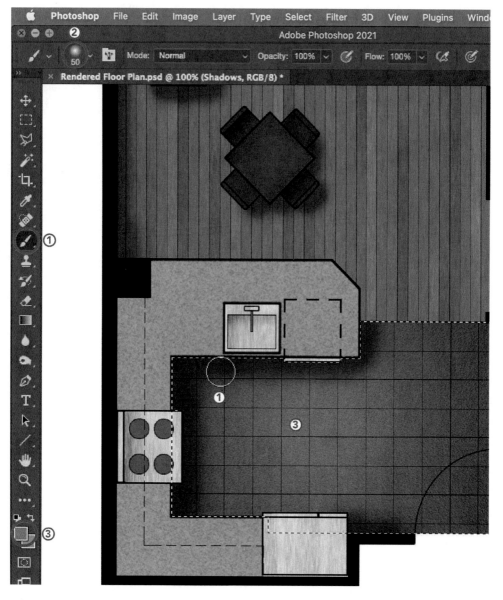

SHADOWS ON LIGHT SURFACES

For white and light surfaces you will need to use a ①**darker color** in order for the shadow to show.

For the bedroom shadows a ②**warm grey** was used and the bathroom a ③**cool grey**.

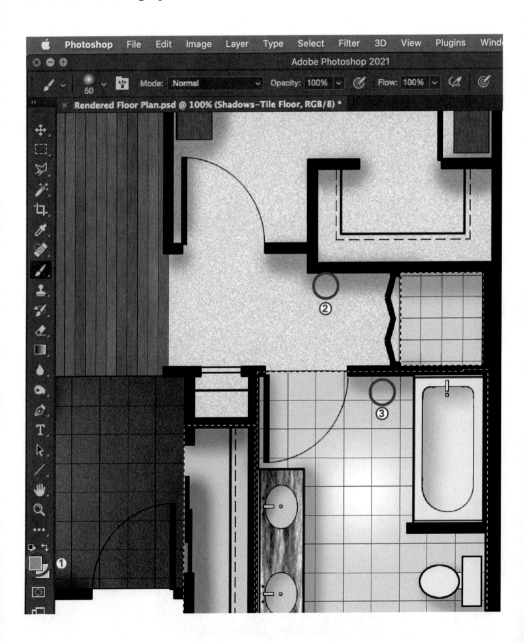

6

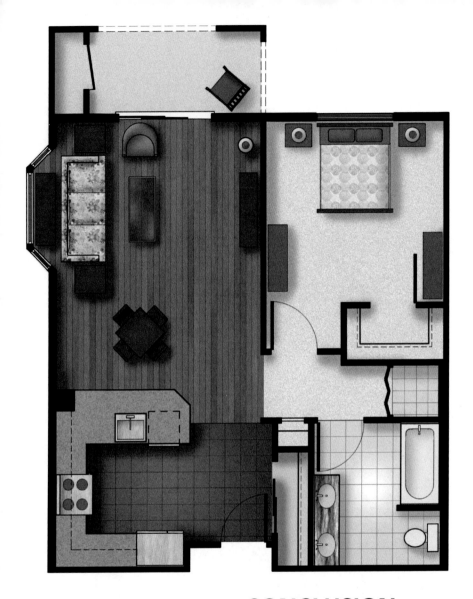

CONCLUSION

Using the step-by-step approach used in this book, you will be able to further develop your professional rendering skills. I have demonstrated options to render a variety of materials and objects using Photoshop. The completed rendering of the floor plan, using all of the techniques shown in this book, is shown above.

Photoshop is a powerful application with many uses for students and design professionals. Many of the techniques shown in this book can be used for rendering other materials by simply changing colors, noise levels, and/or filter options. The more you use Photoshop, the more proficient you will become. Happy rendering!

ABOUT THE AUTHOR

Robert H. Frank is a freelance architectural illustrator in Napa, California. In addition, he teaches digital and traditional rendering techniques at the Academy of Art University in San Francisco as well as workshops. Robert is a graduate of the Rhode Island School of Design with a degree in architecture. He is a past president of the American Society of Architectural Illustrators (ASAI). Follow Robert on Instagram @robertfrank.illustration

RESOURCES

Floor Plan and Patterns Used in This Book
rfassoc.com/book.html

Seamless Textures
Textures.com
SketchUpTextureClub.com
Google.com - Image search - Seamless fabric textures

Photoshop
helpx.adobe.com/support/photoshop.html

Made in the USA
Monee, IL
01 October 2022

15025847R00057